Imagine 5

WORKBOOK

Fiona Beddall

Teresa Bestwick

COURSE CONSULTANTS

Elaine Boyd

Paul Dummett

Australia • Brazil • Canada • Mexico • Singapore • United Kingdom • United States

National Geographic Learning,
a Cengage Company

***Imagine* 5 Workbook**

Authors: Fiona Beddall, Teresa Bestwick

Course Consultants: Elaine Boyd, Paul Dummett

Publisher: Rachael Gibbon

Executive Editor: Joanna Freer

Project Manager: Natalie Roberts

Editorial Assistant: Polly McLachlan

Director of Global Marketing: Ian Martin

Product Marketing Manager: Fernanda De Oliveira

Heads of Strategic Marketing:

Charlotte Ellis (Europe, Middle East and Africa)

Justin Kaley (Asia and Greater China)

Irina Pereyra (Latin America)

Senior Content Project Manager: Beth McNally

Senior Media Researcher: Leila Hishmeh

Senior Art Director: Brenda Carmichael

Operations Support: Rebecca G. Barbush, Hayley Chwazik-Gee

Manufacturing Manager: Eyvett Davis

Composition: Composure

ISBN: 978-0-357-91186-0

National Geographic Learning
Cheriton House, North Way,
Andover, Hampshire, SP10 5BE
United Kingdom

Locate your local office at **international.cengage.com/region**

Visit National Geographic Learning online at **ELTNGL.com**
Visit our corporate website at **www.cengage.com**

Printed in the United Kingdom by Ashford Colour Press
Print Number: 01 Print Year: 2022

MIX
Paper from responsible sources
FSC® C011748

Imagine 5 WORKBOOK

Welcome 4
1 Move to the Music! 6
2 Cool Clothes 12
Units 1–2 Let's Talk p. 18, Video p. 19, Review p. 20
3 The Past 22
4 Fresh Food 28
Units 3–4 Game p. 34, Reading Challenge p. 35, Review p. 36
5 Imagine the Future 38
6 Feeling Great! 44
Units 5–6 Let's Talk p. 50, Video p. 51, Review p. 52
7 The City 54
8 You Can Do It! 60
Units 7–8 Game p. 66, Reading Challenge p. 67, Review p. 68
Word List 70

A **These four men work in the National Park.** Who is Mr Place?
Read the description and tick the box.

a. ☐

c. ☐

b. ☐

d. ☐

Mr Place has got dark hair. It's curly and it isn't very long. He's got a round face and a dark beard, but he hasn't got a moustache. He's short. He isn't the thinnest man, but he's very strong.

B **Write a description of one of the other men in Activity A.**

____

____

____

C Listen and tick the correct answer. TR: 0.1

1. What does the boy like doing at the weekend?

a.  ☐ b.  ☐ c. ☐

2. Where does the girl like going on holiday?

a.  ☐ b.  ☐ c. ☐

3. What does the girl like having to eat when she goes to the café?

a.  ☐ b.  ☐ c. ☐

D Answer the questions.

1. Are you and your family going to a theme park this weekend?

   No, we're not.

2. Are you going to go canoeing in the evening?

   ____

3. Is your mum going to visit a museum tomorrow?

   ____

4. Is your dad going to sleep in a tent this weekend?

   ____

5. Are you and your family going to eat outside this evening?

   ____

1 Move to the Music!

Lesson 1 Vocabulary

A Look and complete.

1. 
2.
3. 
4.
5. 
6.
7. 
8. 
9.

What's the secret word? ____________ music

B Listen and write T (true) or F (false). TR: 1.1

1. The girl wants to go to a concert on Saturday. ______
2. Z Machines are a music group from Spain. ______
3. Z Machines play classical music. ______
4. A robot named Cosmo plays the keyboard. ______
5. A robot named Ashura plays the drums. ______
6. There aren't any singers or dancers at the concert. ______

C Design your own music robot. Draw and write about it.

My robot's name is ____________.

____________ can ____________

____________.

____________ usually plays

____________ music.

A **Complete the text with the verbs in parentheses.** Use the past simple.

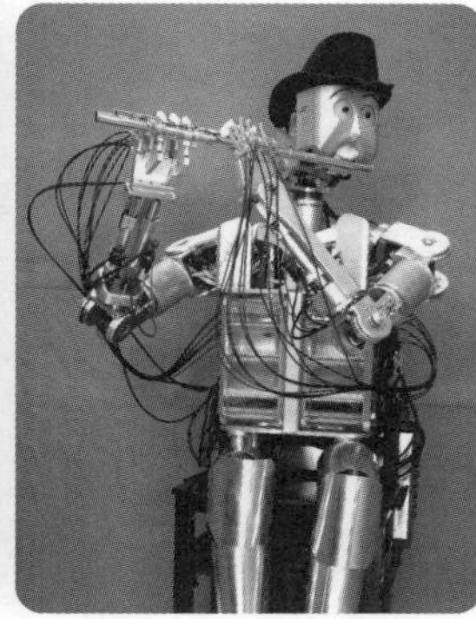

Yesterday, I 1. ________________ (watch) some music videos. In the first video, there 2. ________________ (be) a robot with a violin, but I 3. ________________ (not like) the music very much. Then a robot 4. ________________ (play) some very fast music on the flute. I 5. ________________ (love) it! In the last video, the robot 6. ________________ (not play) an instrument. It 7. ________________ (move) its arms and an orchestra 8. ________________ (play) the music. All three robots 9. ________________ (be) amazing!

B **Listen and circle the correct answer.** TR: 1.2

1. The girl *played / didn't play* a computer game on Saturday.

2. The robots in the video *danced / didn't dance* to classical music.

3. The girl thinks the dancing *was / wasn't* amazing.

4. The robots *were / weren't* very big.

5. The robots *moved / didn't move* like real people.

C **Complete the questions in the past simple.** Listen again and write the answers. TR: 1.3

1. ________________ the video at a basketball game? (the girl, watch)

____

2. ________________ in the UK? (the robots, be)

____

3. ________________ the music? (the girl, like)

____

4. ________________ in the same way? (all the robots, dance)

____

A **Complete the text with these verbs.**

banged carried climbed shouted

There was a show about some incredible dancers from India. In Odisha, the dancers 1. ______________ 'Haido!' when the singer was quiet. In Rajasthan, some dancers 2. ______________ eight bowls on their heads! The musicians 3. ______________ their drums for the dance. They were very loud. In Karnataka, the dancers 4. ______________ onto drums!

B **Read.** Complete the text with the sentences (a–d).

a. Then they banged their drums quickly.
b. You can watch these dancers playing their drums in one of our programmes.
c. We wanted to learn more about dance and music in India, and we wanted to make a film.
d. They wear colourful costumes and many of them play the drums.

Indian Music and Dance

My name is Soumik Datta. My brother, Souvid, is a photographer. We live in England, but we were born in India. 1. ________. So, in 2015, we visited India and saw more than 100 different musicians. One group of musicians from Karnataka is famous for its dance called 'The Kunitha'. 2. ________ They sing and jump too. All the men are farmers, but they love dancing.

We filmed their show. It was incredible! The dancers carried big drums and they banged them loudly. They all shouted and they kicked their feet. Then they played their drums quietly and some of the dancers climbed onto the drums to make a tower.
3. ________ It was very exciting.

4. ________ We hope you enjoy it!

C **Read the text again.** Answer the questions.

1. Where do Soumik and Souvid Datta live? ______________
2. Which country did they visit in 2015? ______________
3. Do the farmers like doing the Kunitha dance? ______________
4. What instrument did the Karnataka musicians play? ______________
5. Did Soumik enjoy the Kunitha dance? ______________

A Complete the text with the adverbs of the words in parentheses.

One of my favourite Indian dances is the Bhavai dance. At the beginning, the musicians play their music 1. ________________ (quiet), and a dancer puts a bowl on her head. Then another person helps the dancer. This person puts a second bowl 2. ________________ (careful) on top of the first bowl, so there are two bowls on the dancer's head. Then the helper puts on a third bowl, a fourth, a fifth and sometimes more. When the dancer has lots of bowls on her head, the musicians play 3. ________________ (loud). The dancer walks 4. ________________ (slow) and moves her arms 5. ________________ (quick). It's amazing! Some Bhavai dancers can dance 6. ________________ (good) with ten bowls on their heads! Lots of people come to this part of India to watch this amazing dance.

B Look and complete the sentences with adverbs.

1. It's moving ________________.

2. She's talking ________________.

3. He's playing the drums ________________.

4. He can't walk very ________________.

C Complete the sentences about you. Use the adverbs of the words in the box.

bad	careful	good	loud	quick	quiet	slow

1. I usually run ________________ in PE.
2. I don't like singing ________________.
3. I usually talk ________________ in class.
4. I can ride a bike ________________.
5. I usually eat my dinner ________________.

Lesson 5 Writing

A **Complete the chart about going on a picnic with your family.** Use the information below.

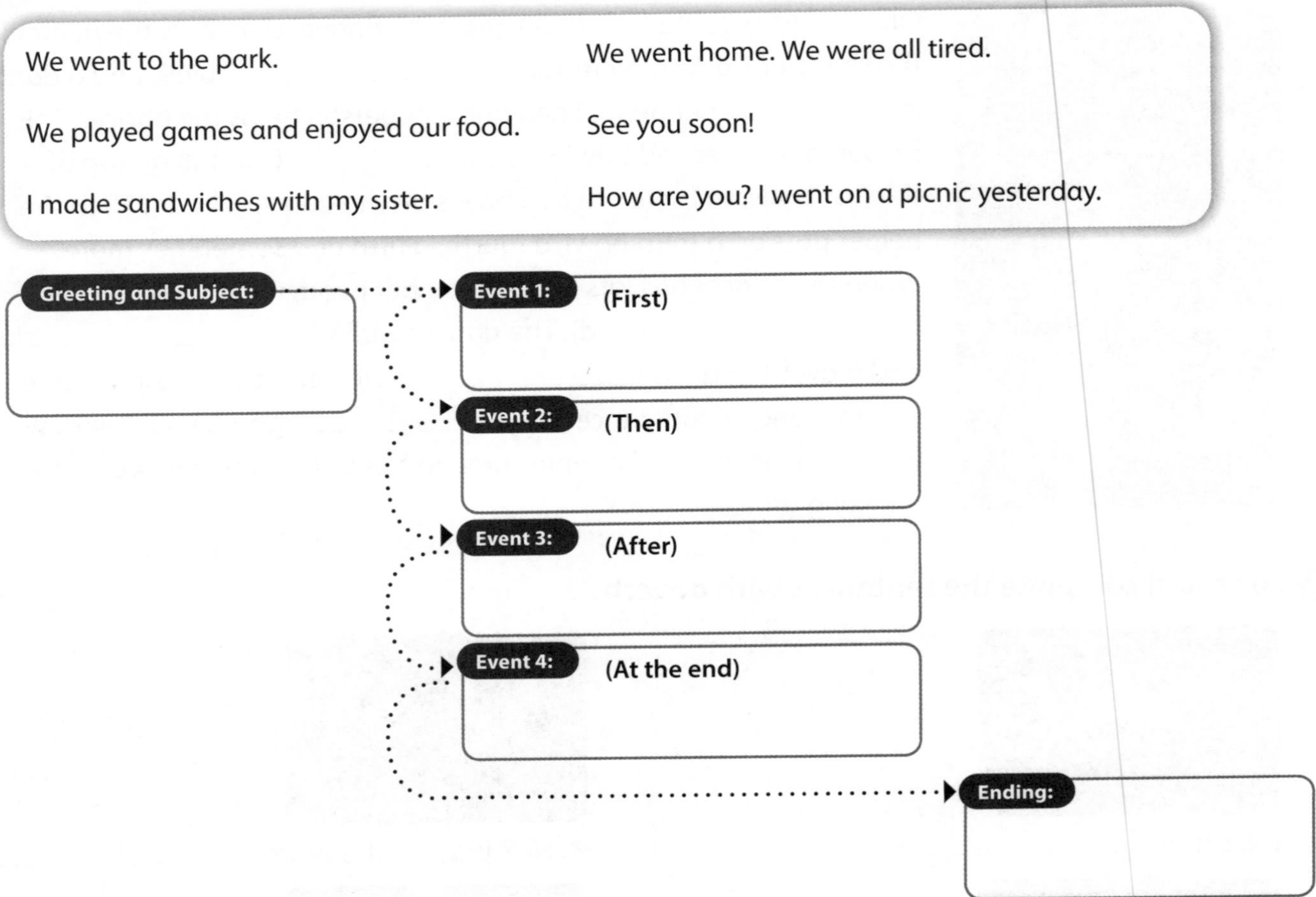

B **Use your chart from the Unit 1 Writing Lesson to help you write an email to a friend about your weekend.**

From: ______________

To: ______________

Subject: ______________________________

Hi ______________ ,

How are you? Yesterday was ____.

First, ____.

Then, ____.

After ______________ , ______________________________.

At the end, ____.

See you soon!

____

Send

A **Read and circle the best answer for you.**

1. Which is your favourite place for dancing?
   a. My bedroom, because people can't see me there.
   b. Performances, because everyone is watching me.
   c. Parties, because my friends and I can do the same dance together.
   d. Dance class, because we learn new ways to dance.
2. What do you do when a friend does an unusual free-time activity?
   a. I laugh because unusual activities aren't very cool.
   b. I ask about it because I want to know more.
   c. I want to do the activity too.
   d. I want to try it too, but I worry that people will laugh at me.
3. Do you and your friends like the same things?
   a. No. We're different people and we like different things.
   b. Sometimes, but we like different things too.
   c. Usually. Maybe that's why we're friends.
   d. Yes. We can't be friends if we like different things.

B **Circle the best answer.**

1. *Dance / Don't dance* however you want.
2. *Be / Don't be* kind when your friends try something new.
3. *Laugh / Don't laugh* at people because they're different from you.
4. *Always / Don't always* do the same things as your friends.

C **Play a song and dance however you want.** When you finish, complete the sentences about you.

I danced ______________. It was ______________ to dance like this.

I was ______________ while I was dancing.

2 Cool Clothes

Lesson 1 Vocabulary

A **Look and read.** Write the correct words.

a pocket	comfortable	plain	striped	sunglasses

1. You can carry keys and small toys in this part of your clothes. __________
2. This is a design with lines of different colours. __________
3. These clothes feel good when you wear them. __________
4. You wear these to protect your eyes on sunny days. __________
5. This describes something that is only one colour. __________

B **Listen, colour and write.** TR: 2.1

C **Complete the sentences about you.**

1. I like wearing __________ and __________.
2. I don't often wear __________.
3. I never wear __________.
4. My most comfortable clothes are my __________ and my __________.

A Colour the words that complete the question below. What's the secret picture?

Whose are these clothes? Are they ______________________ ?

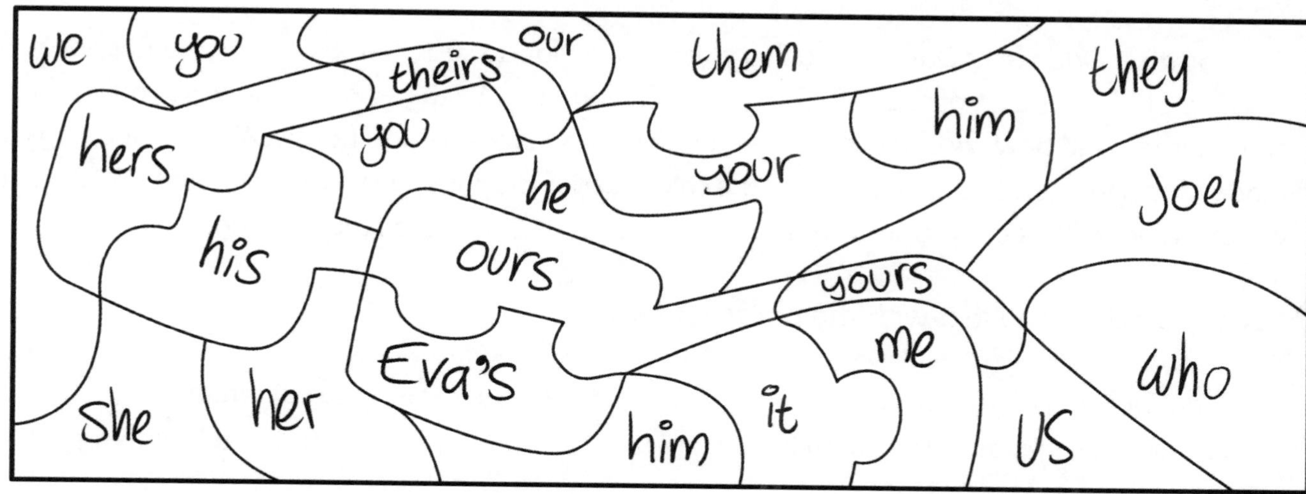

B Complete the conversations with possessive pronouns.

1. **A:** Are those trainers Tom's?
   B: Yes, I think they're ______________________ .
2. **A:** Whose is that striped hat?
   B: It's ______________________ . I bought it last week.
3. **A:** I thought these sunglasses were Lucia's, but she says they're not ______________________ . Are they ______________________ ?
   B: No, they aren't mine.
4. **A:** Wow! Whose big car is that?
   B: It's ______________________ . There are seven people in our family.
5. **A:** Is this Giorgia and Matteo's house?
   B: No, that one's ______________________ , opposite the café.

C Answer the questions. Use possessive pronouns.

1. Our English book is yellow. What about yours?
   Ours is ____
2. There are three people in my family. How many are there in yours?
   ____
3. My best friend's favourite sport is football. What's your best friend's favourite sport?
   ____

Lesson 3 Reading

A **Complete the text with these words.**

weak   match   frighten   hurt

The day after Odd Socks Day, our teacher asked us, 'What do superheroes do when bad people 1. __________ or 2. __________ others?' We talked about how we could be like superheroes, and how we could keep everyone at our school safe and happy. We wore leggings and made masks to 3. __________ the colour of our leggings. We were all superheroes! And now we know: none of us are too small or too 4. __________ to stop bullying.

B **Read.** Complete the text with the phrases (a–d).

a. stop bullying at school
b. wear two socks that don't match
c. celebrate being different
d. being different is not a bad thing

Odd Socks Day

Each November in the UK, there is a special day called Odd Socks Day. It's very easy to take part. When you get dressed in the morning, all you have to do is 1. __________, along with your usual clothes. Then you go to school!

People usually wear socks to keep their feet warm. Socks usually come in a pair. So why do people wear odd socks on this day? Because odd socks have a message! The message of Odd Socks Day is to show that 2. __________. Everyone is special and unique.

Sometimes, bullies frighten or hurt children because they are different. Sometimes, older and stronger children bully younger children. They make the mistake of thinking because they are younger and smaller, they are weaker. It is very important to 3. __________. Everyone needs to feel happy and safe.

On Odd Socks Day, children 4. __________! What odd socks would you wear on Odd Socks Day?

C **Read the text again.** Circle the correct answers.

1. Socks usually *have a message* / *keep feet warm*.
2. The message of Odd Socks Day is that *it's good to be different* / *socks are important*.
3. It's important that everyone feels *scared* / *safe* at school.

A Complete the sentences with these words.

to buy | to catch | ~~to hold~~ | to learn | to make | to play

1. I like having a pocket in my coat ___to hold___ my keys.
2. I walked to the bus stop ____________ a bus.
3. I went to the shopping centre ____________ some new trainers.
4. I needed the trainers ____________ volleyball.
5. I'm on a volleyball team ____________ new friends.
6. I practise volleyball every week ____________ how to play better.

B Mo Bridges makes bow ties. Listen and write T (true) or F (false). TR: 2.2

1. Mo chose his clothes to feel comfortable. ________
2. He went to the shop to look for his grandma. ________
3. Mo put photos of his bow ties on the Internet to sell them. ________
4. He went on TV to talk about his bow ties. ________
5. He went to the White House to meet the president of the United States. ________

Mo Bridges wearing one of his bow ties

C Complete with your own ideas. Use infinitives of purpose.

1. People wear sun hats in the summer ___to keep their heads cool___.
2. People go to cafés ____________.
3. People do sports ____________.
4. I go to school ____________.
5. I go to the park ____________.
6. I go to my friend's house ____________.

Lesson 5 Writing

A **Complete the chart using the information from the box.**

11 a.m. to 2 p.m.	8th July	Pool party
7 Park Road	To Carla	Bring your swimming costume

Who?	
What?	
When?	
Where?	
What else?	

B **Use your chart from the Unit 2 Writing Lesson to help you write an invitation for a friend.**

To: ____________

____

When: ______________________________

Where: ______________________________

Please come to my ______________________________

____

______________________________.

Don't forget ______________________________

______________________________.

Email ______________________________.

VALUE

Look after your things.

A **Which pictures show people looking after things?** Look and tick.

1. 

☐

2.  ☐

3.  ☐

4.  ☐

5.  ☐

6.  ☐

B **Draw something that's special to you.** Then answer the questions.

1. What is it?

____

____

____

2. Where did it come from?

____

____

____

3. Why is it special to you?

____

____

____

4. How do you look after it?

____

____

____

A **Look at the conversation.** For each question, circle the correct answer. Then listen and check. TR: 2.3

1. **Shop assistant:** Hello. Can I help you?
   Customer:
   a. Yes, please. When is the party?
   b. Yes, please. I'm looking for a new skirt.
   c. I'm wearing a striped T-shirt.
2. **Shop assistant:** OK. What size are you?
   Customer:
   a. The skirt is for my sister, and she's size 34.
   b. I would like a red and blue skirt.
   c. That's very expensive!
3. **Shop assistant:** What colour would you like?
   Customer:
   a. I don't like it.
   b. Blue and white – they're my sister's favourite colours.
   c. Perfect! My sister loves skirts!
4. **Shop assistant:** Here's a nice skirt. Do you like it?
   Customer:
   a. I'm a size 34. How much is it, please?
   b. It's a blue coat.
   c. It's perfect! How much is it, please?
5. **Shop assistant:** It's 25 euros.
   Customer:
   a. Oh, that's very big!
   b. It's very cold.
   c. I'll take it!

B **Complete the conversation.**

A: Hello. 1. ______________________________

B: Yes, please. I'm looking for a new coat.

A: 2. ______________________________

B: Green or black, please.

A: 3. ______________________________

B: I'm usually a medium.

A: Here you are.

B: Ooh, I like it. It's very nice.
4. ______________________________

A: It's 79 euros.

B: 5. ______________________________

A **Tick the things you saw in the video.**

B **Answer the questions about Nick Nichols.**

1. What's Nick's job?

____

____

2. Where does Nick work?

____

____

3. Why does he wear special clothes?

____

____

4. Why does he take photos of nature?

____

____

C **Imagine you're a wildlife photographer.** Look at the photo. Answer the questions using the words from the box.

cave	fly	nighttime

1. Where does the animal live?

____

2. When is the best time to take the photo?

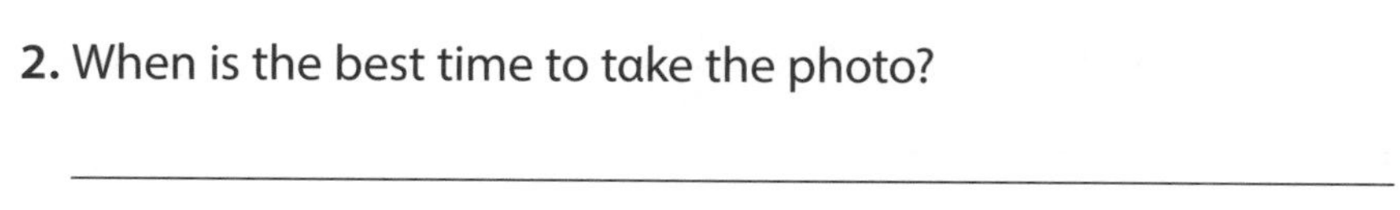

____

3. What is the animal doing in the photo?

____

A **Find nine words about music.**

c	d	o	y	o	p	u	l	i
e	k	e	y	b	o	a	r	d
l	v	k	e	c	p	l	s	a
l	i	d	r	u	m	a	i	n
o	o	s	s	i	u	c	n	c
f	l	u	t	e	s	a	g	e
l	i	m	u	s	i	i	e	r
c	n	c	o	n	c	e	r	t

Write the extra letters to find the question. Then write your answer.

____________________________________?

____

B **Read, choose and write.**

cello concert flute popular trainers striped

1. These are a type of shoe you wear to do sports. ____________
2. This is a public performance of music. ____________
3. Zebras' and tigers' fur is ... ____________
4. This is a large musical instrument with strings. ____________
5. This is what something is when lots of people like it. ____________
6. You play it by blowing over a hole and pressing its keys. ____________

C **Complete the sentences with the verbs.** Use the past simple.

be (x3) dance listen look play

The school party 1. ____________ great. There 2. ____________ lots of pizza and fruit punch. We 3. ____________ lots of games and there 4. ____________ prizes too! We 5. ____________ to pop music and our teacher 6. ____________ with all the students – she 7. ____________ very happy!

D Write the adverbs.

1. loud ____________
2. bad ____________
3. quick ____________
4. slow ____________
5. careful ____________
6. good ____________

E Whose clothes are these? Listen and write a letter in each box. TR: 2.4

1. Dad ☐
2. Jane ☐
3. Susan ☐
4. Tom ☐

a.

b.

c.

d.

e.

f.

F Answer the questions with your own ideas. Use infinitives of purpose.

1. Why do some people wear odd socks?

____

2. Why do people wear trainers when they do sports?

____

3. Why do people wear sunglasses?

____

4. Why do people need pockets in clothes?

____

3 The Past

Lesson 1 Vocabulary

A **Look and write the words.**

1. 
a key

2.  

3.  

4. 

5. 

6. 

7. 

8. 

B **Listen to the description.** Write T (true) or F (false). TR: 3.1

1. Yuka lives on the 13th floor. ________
2. There's a family living upstairs with a big dog. ________
3. Yuka sometimes sees her neighbours in the lift. ________
4. Yuka's house in the countryside had a grey roof. ________
5. Her bedroom was downstairs, next to the kitchen. ________
6. She played football in the front garden with her brother. ________

C **Draw and write about the building you live in.** Use five or more words from Activity A.

My name's ________________ and I live in

a(n) ____________ in ________________.

We live ______________________________

____

______________________________________.

A Tick the verbs that don't belong.

1. ☐ talk ☐ listen ☐ wait ... to
2. ☐ wait ☐ look ☐ talk ... for
3. ☐ talk ☐ listen ☐ think ... about
4. ☐ think ☐ travel ☐ look ... at

B Complete the text. Use *about, to, at* or *for.*

Last summer, I travelled [1] ________________ Egypt with my family. It was a great holiday, but we had some problems. First, we had to wait [2] ________________ a long time in the airport and it was really boring. Then my headphones broke, so I couldn't listen [3] ________________ music on the plane. One day, we went to see the pyramids in Giza – they were incredible! But my sister lost her camera and we had to look [4] ________________ it for a long time. Then another day, my mum and dad talked [5] ________________ going for a camel ride, but it was very expensive so we went [6] ________________ a museum. We looked [7] ________________ old objects for hours! On the last day, we went on a boat on the Nile River and a man talked [8] ________________ us about the crocodiles that swim in the river. It was really interesting. They are huge with very big, scary teeth!

C Complete the questions. Use *to, about* or *at.*

1. What type of music do you like listening ________________?
2. What do you talk ________________ with your friends?
3. What animals do you like looking ________________ in the wild?

D Answer the questions in Activity C about you.

1. ____
2. ____
3. ____

A **Read and circle the correct answers.**

1. Marbles are often made of *glass / chalk.*
2. You have to hit other marbles out of the *circle / squares.*
3. We play games on the *pavement / glass* outside our house.
4. Use *chalk / pavement* to write numbers when you play games outside.
5. When you play hopscotch, you need to draw ten *circles / squares.*

B **Read.** Complete the text with the sentences (a–f).

Playing Games Outside

Sixty or seventy years ago, many children played games on the pavement near their houses. They didn't have computer games or TV, so they had to make their own games outside. 1. ________ Why don't you try these traditional games too?

Marbles Children played marbles in Roman times nearly 2,000 years ago! Marbles are small glass or clay balls. 2. ________ You have to throw your marble to hit other marbles out of the circle.

Hopscotch 3. ________ In Argentina, it is called *rayuela* and in Malaysia, it is called *ketingting*. First, you have to draw squares and numbers with chalk. 4. ________, and hopping and jumping on the squares.

Elastics 5. ________ Two children have to stand with a long circle of elastic around their legs. Another child jumps and makes shapes with the elastic using their feet. 6. ________

a. All the children sing a song at the same time.
b. Then, you take turns throwing a small stone
c. They had fun playing together with their friends.
d. This game started in China in the seventh century.
e. This is an old game from Roman times too.
f. You usually draw a circle with chalk.

C **Read the text again.** Write T (true) or F (false).

1. Children sing when they play with marbles. ________
2. Marbles are usually made of glass or clay. ________
3. Marbles and hopscotch are Roman games. ________
4. You need a small stone to play hopscotch. ________
5. In Malaysia, hopscotch is called *rayuela*. ________
6. Children started to play elastics in the 17th century. ________

A **Complete the rules about a game.** Write *have to* or *has to*. Then tick the correct picture.

Marco Polo

You usually play this game in a swimming pool with lots of friends. One person [1.] ______________ wear something to cover his eyes. He [2.] ______________ catch somebody. All the other children [3.] ______________ swim around him. That person [4.] ______________ say 'Marco', then all the children [5.] ______________ say 'Polo'. The person who can't see [6.] ______________ listen carefully to know where the others are and catch somebody. If he catches you, you [7.] ______________ cover your eyes.

1. ☐

2. ☐

3. ☐

B **Listen to a boy describing a game from Activity A.** Write the correct number. TR: 3.2

He's describing Picture ________.

C **Listen again.** Correct the sentences. TR: 3.3

1. Miguel had to catch his friends. ______________________________
2. The children had to sit down. ______________________________
3. The children didn't have to run fast. ______________________________
4. Simon had to go through Miguel's legs. ______________________________

Lesson 5 Writing

A **Complete the timeline with information from the box.**

Today	No games were held in the Colosseum	80
The Arch of Constantine was added	1990	

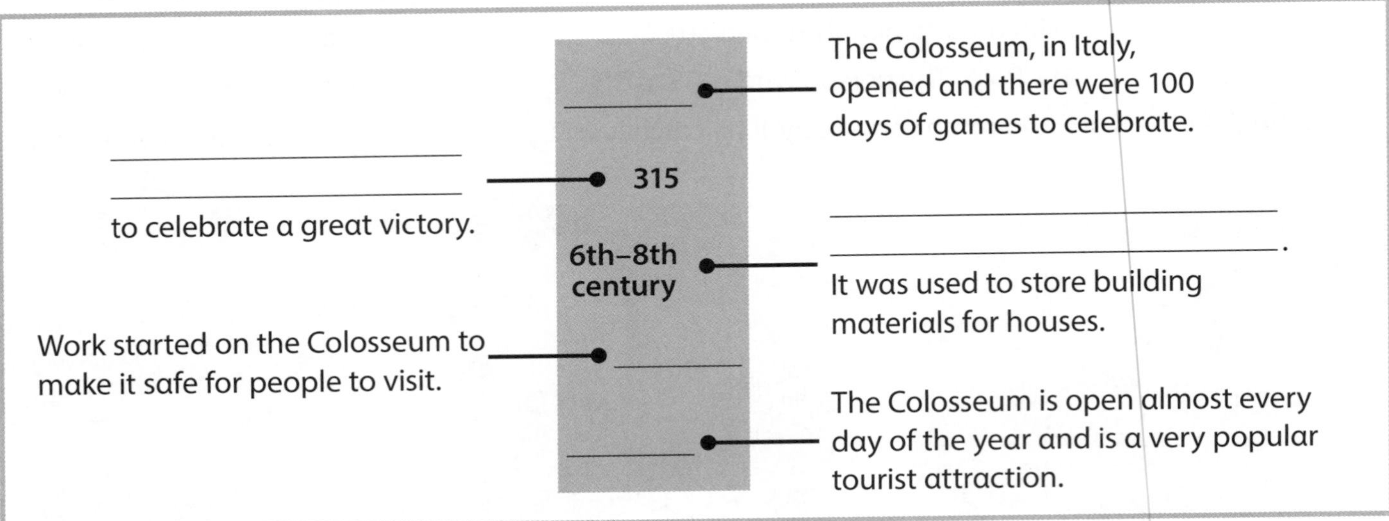

B **Use your timeline from the Unit 3 Writing Lesson to help you makes notes about an important building and its past.**

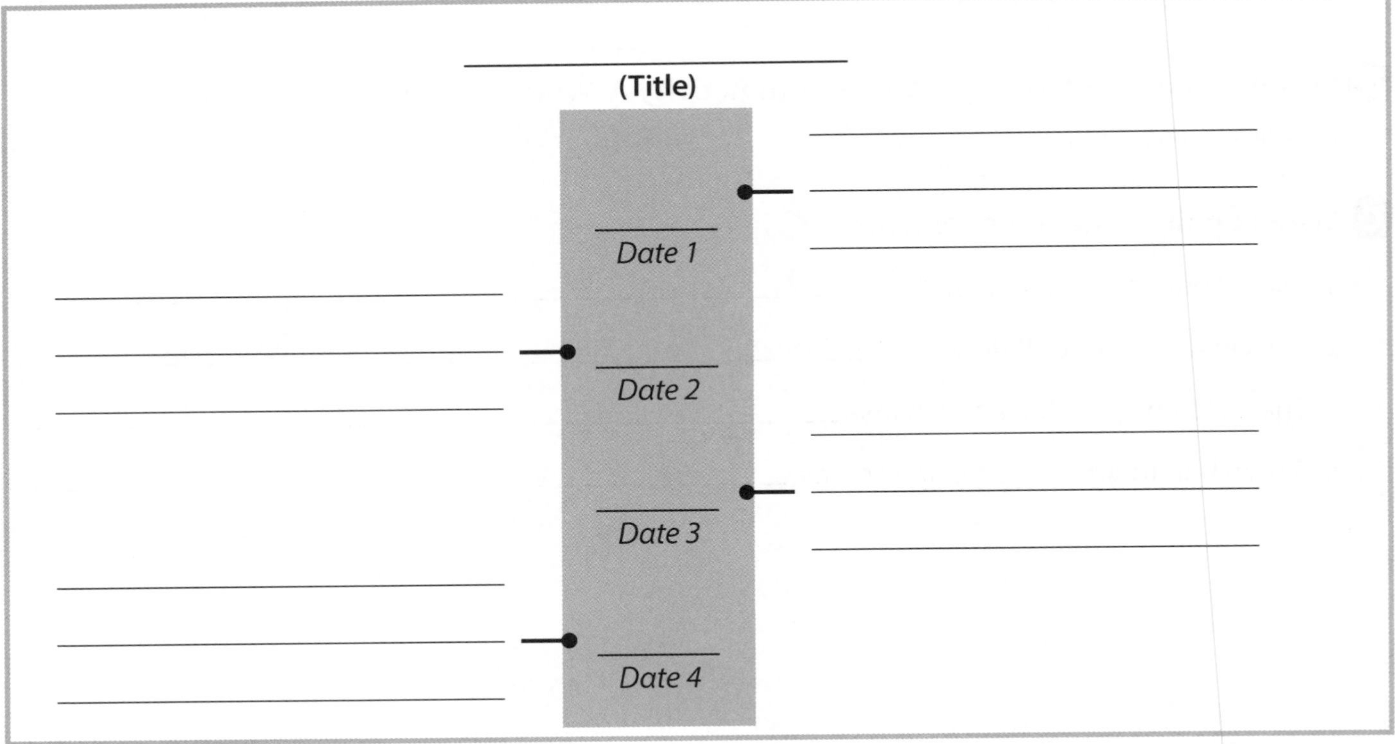

A Read. Circle the best answers for you.

1. I am grateful for my good health, family and friends.
   a. Always
   b. Sometimes
   c. Never
2. I am grateful for basic things like food, clothing and shelter.
   a. Always
   b. Sometimes
   c. Never
3. I am grateful whenever I receive help from someone.
   a. Always
   b. Sometimes
   c. Never
4. When I am feeling unhappy, I remind myself of the good things in my life.
   a. Always
   b. Sometimes
   c. Never

B Why is it important to be grateful? Tick the answers you think are true.

- [ ] It makes me happy.
- [ ] It helps to improve relationships.
- [ ] It makes people like me more.
- [ ] It helps me to reduce stress.
- [ ] It helps me to think more positively.

C Draw a picture of a person you are grateful for. Write why you are grateful.

This is ________________________________

____.

I am grateful because ____________________

____

____.

4 Fresh Food

Lesson 1 Vocabulary

A Complete with *a*, *e*, *i*, o and *u*.

1. br__cc__l__

2. c__r__ __l

3. a ch__ll__

4. sw__ __tc__rn

5. j__m

6. l__tt__c__

7. n__ts

8. __l__v__s

B Answer the questions. Use the words from Activity A.

1. Which are fruit and vegetables? ______________________________
2. Which do people often eat for breakfast? ______________________________
3. Which do people sometimes eat as a snack? ______________________________

C Listen to a girl talking about her holiday. Choose the correct answer. TR: 4.1

1. What did she have for breakfast?

a. 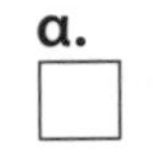  b. 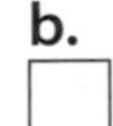  c. 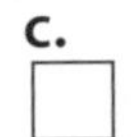 

2. What fruit did she eat at the beach?

a. 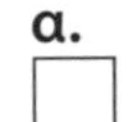    b.    c.   

3. What did she have for dinner?

a.    b. 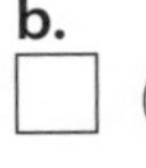 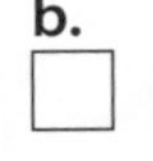 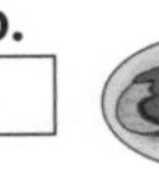  c. 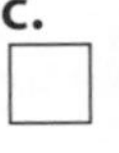 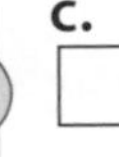 

4. What food did she like?

a.   b. 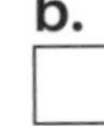  c. 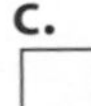 

A **Complete the questions with *How much* or *How many*.**

1. ______________ courgettes are there?
2. ______________ toast is there?
3. ______________ cereal is there?
4. ______________ milk is there?
5. ______________ eggs are there?
6. ______________ orange juice is there?

B **Look at the picture and answer the questions from Activity A.**

1. ______________
2. ______________
3. ______________
4. ______________
5. ______________
6. ______________

C **Put the questions in order.**

1. go to / How / the show / many people / ?

____

2. many / are there / contests / How / ?

____

3. much / How / weigh / did the / heaviest carrot / ?

____

4. much / heaviest pumpkin / How / weigh / did the / ?

____

D **Listen.** Answer the questions from Activity C. TR: 4.2

1. ______________
2. ______________
3. ______________
4. ______________

Lesson 3 Reading

A Look and write.

1. s___ ___ ___ ___
2. f___ ___ ___ ___ f___ ___ ___
3. j___ ___ ___ f___ ___ ___
4. w___ ___ ___ ___

B Read and write the best title (a–d) for each paragraph. There is one extra title.

a. How to Grow Vegetables
b. Why You Shouldn't Eat Junk Food
c. A Different Type of Garden
d. Good Reasons to Have a Community Garden

Let's Grow Our Food!

☐ **1.** Fresh food is healthier than junk food, but it's often more expensive. In some towns and cities, people are learning to grow their own fruit and vegetables in community gardens. They share the garden and look after the plants together.

☐ **2.** Ana and her 14-year-old daughter Marjorie live in Quito, Ecuador. Every morning, Ana goes to the community garden. Marjorie often goes with her. Ten families work together in the garden. First, they plant seeds and they water the plants. They pull out weeds and pick the vegetables when they're ready. It's hard work, but they grow lots of food! They eat a lot of the vegetables and they sell some at the market too.

☐ **3.** Ana enjoys sharing this garden because it brings people together. The children love working outside and watching the vegetables grow. They are also eating more healthily now. 'I didn't like vegetables before,' Marjorie says, 'but now I like to eat lots of sweetcorn and potatoes. They're delicious and they come from our garden.'

C Read the text again. Write T (true) or F (false).

1. It's always cheaper to eat fresh food than junk food. ________

2. There are people from different families working in the community garden. ________

3. Ana has to work hard to grow vegetables. ________

4. Ana and Marjorie eat all the vegetables they grow. ________

5. Marjorie likes eating vegetables from their garden. ________

A Read and circle the correct answer.

Girl: Hi, Dad. What's up?

Dad: I'm in the supermarket and I forgot the shopping list. How [1.] *many / much* milk is there?

Girl: There's [2.] *a little / a few* milk in this bottle and there are two more bottles in the fridge.

Dad: OK, so we don't need milk. And how [3.] *many / much* cheese is there?

Girl: There isn't [4.] *some / any* cheese.

Dad: OK, and what about lettuce?

Girl: There's [5.] *lots of / any* lettuce. Mum bought some yesterday. But there aren't [6.] *some / any* tomatoes.

Dad: OK. And carrots?

Girl: There are [7.] *a few / a little* carrots. Can you buy sweets too? [8.] *A little / Lots of* sweets?

Dad: I can buy [9.] *a few / any* sweets.

B Look at the picture in Activity A and write sentences. Use *a little, a few, lots of* and *any.*

1. (apples) ______________________
2. (grapes) ______________________
3. (juice) ______________________
4. (eggs) ______________________
5. (pasta) ______________________

C Write sentences about the food in your kitchen.

1. (any) There isn't any lettuce in our fridge.
2. (any) ______________________
3. (some) ______________________
4. (a few) ______________________
5. (a little) ______________________
6. (lots of) ______________________

Lesson 5 Writing

A Complete the chart with information from the recipe.

Banana Maple Ice Cream

Ingredients

- 4 bananas (peeled and sliced)
- 125 ml milk
- 30 ml (2 tbsp) maple syrup

Instructions

1. First, place the banana slices separately on a tray.
2. Next, freeze the banana slices for 30 minutes.
3. Then, remove from the freezer. Put the banana slices in a blender. Add the milk and maple syrup.
4. Finally, blend until creamy. Serve immediately in a bowl.

Ingredients
How many? How much? (ml, kg, etc.)

Instructions
(How long? Serve how?)

1.
2.
3.
4.

B Use your chart from the Unit 4 Writing Lesson to help you write a recipe for a meal or drink you like. Draw a picture of your completed recipe.

____
(Recipe Name)

Ingredients

- ____________ • ____________ • ____________
- ____________ • ____________ • ____________

Instructions

1. ______________________________
2. ______________________________
3. ______________________________
4. ______________________________

VALUE

Make your own food.

A Why do people make their own food? Tick the best answers.

1. It's healthier than eating junk food. ☐
2. They can buy more biscuits and sweets when they go shopping. ☐
3. They can use fresh ingredients. ☐
4. They know what ingredients are in their food. ☐
5. It's more expensive than eating in a restaurant. ☐
6. It's good for people who can't eat some food, like bread or nuts. ☐

B Tick the foods that your family makes at home.

pizza	☐	soup	☐	jam	☐
pasta	☐	pancakes	☐	chips	☐
sandwiches	☐	curry	☐	dumplings	☐
pies	☐	milkshakes	☐	rice	☐

C Read about a boy who makes his own food. Then write about how you help your family in the kitchen. Draw a picture.

After school, I help my mother make *chips mayai*. It's a dish from my country, Kenya. We go to the market and buy the ingredients. First, I cut the potatoes into pieces. Next, we cook the potatoes with eggs, and finally, we make a sauce with fresh tomatoes and chillis. It's delicious, cheap and quick to make!

After school, I ______________________.

It's a dish ______________________.

We go to ______________________.

First, ______________________.

Next, ______________________.

Finally, ______________________.

It's ______________________.

A **Find five words for each list and write them on the lines.** How many can you find in the wordsearch?

o	w	s	h	m	a	t	b	d	o
l	e	t	t	u	c	e	r	y	o
i	l	i	u	c	l	s	o	m	e
v	o	r	a	h	i	k	c	e	t
e	t	o	d	c	o	o	c	u	t
s	s	k	d	h	o	w	o	s	d
o	o	a	l	i	t	t	l	e	n
a	f	y	o	u	m	a	i	r	u
n	c	e	r	e	a	l	k	v	t
y	e	i	t	c	o	o	k	e	s

Food

1. ______
2. ______
3. ______
4. ______
5. ______

Amounts

1. ______
2. ______
3. ______
4. ______
5. ______

Actions we do in the kitchen

1. ______
2. ______
3. ______
4. ______
5. ______

B **Use the extra letters from Activity A to write two secret questions.**

______ ______ ______ ______ ______ ______?

______ ______ ______ ______ ______?

C **Answer the questions in Activity B and draw a picture.**

______

______

______

______

______

______

______

The Ancient Maya

A Listen and tick the topics that are mentioned. TR: 4.3

- [ ] where the ancient Maya were from
- [ ] the population size of the ancient Maya
- [ ] the number of people in Maya families
- [ ] what Maya houses were made of
- [ ] what equipment the farmers used
- [ ] what the Maya grew and ate
- [ ] one of the most important Maya discoveries
- [ ] the ingredients in the Maya chocolate drink

B Listen again. Write T (true) or F (false). Then correct the false sentences. TR: 4.4

1. The ancient Maya lived more than 4,000 years ago. ________

2. Most Maya families had five to seven children. ________

3. The men went to work in the fields after lunch. ________

4. Maize was the Maya's most important food. ________

5. The Maya grew and ate many different fruits. ________

6. A pumpkin cost six cacao beans. ________

C Complete the sentences about the text.

1. I was interested to learn that ____

____.

2. I would like to find out more about ____

____.

3. If I were a Maya child, I would ____

____.

A **Look at the picture and complete the text.** There are two extra words.

entrance floors front key lift roof upstairs

Would you like to stay in this incredible treehouse?

There are two [1] ______________ in the treehouse. There's a kitchen and bathroom on the first floor and two small bedrooms [2] ______________. There are windows in the [3] ______________ so you can see the stars from your bed. It's high in the trees, but there isn't a [4] ______________!

Contact Mr Patel to get the [5] ______________.

B **Complete the sentences with *about, to, at* and *for.*** Tick the sentences that are true for you.

1. My family sometimes travels ______________ the mountains for a summer holiday. ☐
2. I have to wait ______________ a bus to go ______________ school. ☐
3. I always think ______________ the future. ☐
4. I like looking ______________ old objects in museums. ☐

C **Listen and complete the information about the school trip.** TR: 4.5

School Trip

Meet:	at the [1] ______________
Can see old maps:	[2] ______________
Have to take:	[3] ______________
Wait for the bus:	at the [4] ______________ of the museum
Food on the bus:	[5] ______________ and orange juice

D **Read the interview with a chef.** Complete it with *have to*, *has to* and *had to*.

Interviewer: When did you start cooking?

Chef: My mum and dad had a small restaurant and when I was young, I [1] ____________ help them in the kitchen. When I was older, I started working in a big restaurant in the city. I [2] ____________ work hard, but I learnt a lot.

Interviewer: Is working in a restaurant fun?

Chef: Yes! I mean, you [3] ____________ get up early to buy fresh ingredients from the market. But you also [4] ____________ invent new recipes, and I like being creative.

Interviewer: Is being the chef the most difficult job in a restaurant?

Chef: I don't know. There are lots of different jobs. The waiter [5] ____________ remember what food people want, and the person in the kitchen washing dishes [6] ____________ work very fast too.

E **Look at the picture and write sentences.** Use each word or phrase from the box once.

a few	a little	any	lots of	some

1. ____
2. ____
3. ____
4. ____
5. ____

5 Imagine the Future

Lesson 1 Vocabulary

A Match. Then write the words.

1.	e-	top	______
2.	head	a tablet	______
3.	lap	book	______
4.	micro	Fi	______
5.	VR	online	______
6.	Wi-	phone	______
7.	charge	whiteboard	______
8.	interactive	phones	______
9.	go	headset	______

B Answer the questions. Use words from Activity A.

1. Which two phrases are actions?

______

2. What does your teacher use in your classroom?

______

3. Which can you use to play games?

______

4. Which pieces of technology do you use at home?

______

5. Which do you use to do homework?

______

C Listen to a conversation about a game. Complete the information. TR: 5.1

Name of the game:	1. ______ Adventures
What Lisa found in the game:	2. ______
What Lisa used to play the game:	3. ______
To play at home, you need:	4. ______ and the app

A Listen to a boy talking about robots. Complete the sentences with *will* or *won't*. TR: 5.2

In the future ...

1. people ______________ go to the supermarket.
2. robots ______________ work in the house.
3. people ______________ have to drive.
4. robots ______________ work as doctors.
5. robots ______________ be police officers.

B Look at the picture. What does the girl think children will do in the year 2120? Complete the sentences. Write *will* or *won't* and the words from the box.

go	have	play	talk	wear	write

1. Children ______________ school uniforms.
2. They ______________ to school in flying cars.
3. They ______________ robot teachers.
4. They ______________ with pencils and pens.
5. They ______________ traditional games outside.
6. They ______________ to friends around the world with VR headsets.

C What do you think children will do in the year 2120? Write sentences using *will* or *won't* and the ideas from the box.

do homework	learn English	play football
read e-books	use VR headsets	watch TV

1. In 2120, children ____.
2. They ____.
3. They ____.
4. They ____.

Lesson 3 Reading

A **Read and complete the sentences.**

control   drop   satellites   send a text

1. The doctors ______________ to people in a medical centre.
2. Pilots ______________ the drones from the medical centre.
3. They use ______________ to tell the drone where to go.
4. The drones ______________ the medicine.

B **Read.** Put the sentences in order.

Flying Machines

Drones are machines that we can control from the ground. They fly, but they don't have pilots. They can carry cameras or other things. In some places, drones have important jobs!

In Rwanda, there are many hills and mountains.

- [ ] **a.** The drone uses satellites to fly to the right place. It drops the box and it flies back.
- [ ] **b.** The people then prepare a box with the medicine and the drone flies it to the doctors.
- [ ] **c.** It takes a long time to travel between villages by car, so doctors use drones to get a delivery of medicine or blood quickly.
- [ ] **d.** They send a text to people in a medical centre in the middle of the country.
- [ ] **e.** They're difficult to find, so the scientists use drones to fly over the forests and take photos.
- [ ] **f.** Will there be more drones in the future? What will they do?
- [ ] **g.** Drones can help wild animals too. In Borneo, scientists want to help and protect orangutans.
- [ ] **h.** They need to study their nests, but the orangutans build them at the top of tall trees.

C **Read the text again.** Write T (true) or F (false).

1. People fly to different places inside the drones. ______
2. In Rwanda, it's faster to travel by car between villages than fly. ______
3. Drones carry medicine and blood to doctors in Rwanda. ______
4. In Borneo, scientists use drones because the orangutans are dangerous. ______
5. The drones take photos of the trees where the orangutans live. ______

A Answer the questions about the future. Write *Yes, there will* or *No, there won't*.

1. Will there be robot actors in films? ______________
2. Will there be drones in your village, town or city? ______________
3. Will there be VR headsets in every house? ______________
4. Will there be Wi-Fi in the jungle and the desert? ______________
5. Will there be interactive whiteboards in every school? ______________

B Read the answers. Write questions with *who*, *what*, *where* and *how*.

1. ____?
   People will live in cities in the clouds in the future.
2. ____?
   I think people will have similar hobbies, like playing football or listening to music.
3. ____?
   People will travel to work by bus, but the bus will have a robot driver.
4. ____?
   Robots will teach people English in the future.
5. ____?
   Robots will clean, cook lunch and take out the rubbish.
6. ____?
   People will go to the moon or Mars on holiday.

C Write questions about the future. Write your answers.

1. Where ____?
   ____
2. Who ____?
   ____
3. What ____?
   ____
4. How ____?
   ____

Lesson 5 Writing

A **Match the parts to form interview questions.** Then complete the chart with the questions.

1. How	a. will people do for work in the future?
2. What	b. much will people's lives change in the future?
3. Why	c. will people start to own robots?
4. Will	d. people's lives change a lot in the future?
5. When	e. will people need to do things differently in the future?

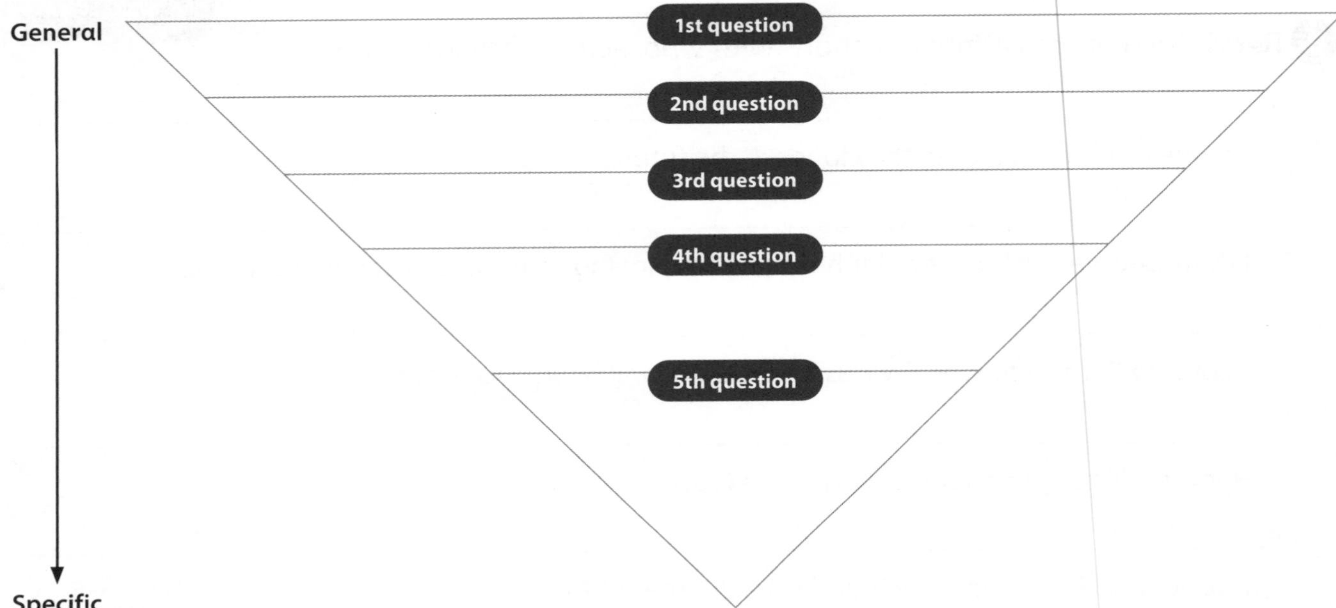

B **Use your notes from the Unit 5 Writing Lesson to help you write your interview.**

An interview with ______________________ **about** ______________________

1st question: ______________________

1st answer: ______________________

2nd question: ______________________

2nd answer: ______________________

3rd question: ______________________

3rd answer: ______________________

4th question: ______________________

4th answer: ______________________

5th question: ______________________

5th answer: ______________________

A Tick the answers that describe you.

How often do you ...	Never	Hardly ever	Sometimes	Often	Every day
1. write stories?	☐	☐	☐	☐	☐
2. draw pictures?	☐	☐	☐	☐	☐
3. invent games with your friends?	☐	☐	☐	☐	☐
4. create songs to sing?	☐	☐	☐	☐	☐
5. think about life in the future?	☐	☐	☐	☐	☐
6. think of different ways to solve a problem?	☐	☐	☐	☐	☐
7. use objects in your house in a different way, for example, a box as a castle?	☐	☐	☐	☐	☐
8. pretend to be someone different, for example, a doctor or an astronaut?	☐	☐	☐	☐	☐

B Read and do the tasks.

Imagine you can have any animal as a pet. Draw a picture.

Imagine you go to a fancy-dress party. Draw your costume.

Imagine you live with a robot in your house. Draw your robot.

Imagine you meet a famous athlete. What would you say?

____

Imagine you see your favourite actor on the street. What would you say?

____

6 Feeling Great!

Lesson 1 Vocabulary

A Write the opposites.

1. asleep ______________ **2.** dark ______________ **3.** take exercise ______________ **4.** strong ______________ **5.** wet ______________

B Complete the sentences. Use words from Activity A.

1. After it rains, the flowers and trees are ______________.

2. My mum is very ______________. She can lift me high in the air!

3. I prefer to sleep in a ______________ room with the door closed.

4. This plant is very ______________. It needs some water to help it grow.

C Listen and draw lines to match. TR: 6.1

Lucas

Harry

Lucy

Oscar

John

D Answer the questions about you.

1. Do you prefer to rest or take exercise after school? Where do you do it?

____

2. What do you do when you're awake at night and can't sleep?

____

A **Complete the sentences to give advice.** Use *should* or *shouldn't* and words from the box.

be	drink	go	rest	stay	wear

Have you got a cold?

1. You ______________ lots of water and hot tea.
2. You ______________ warm clothes.
3. You ______________ to a party.
4. You ______________ and watch films on the sofa.
5. You ______________ near babies or old people.
6. You ______________ at home until you are better.

B **Listen to the conversation.** What's the problem? Tick the correct answer. TR: 6.2

- [ ] **a.** She arrived late to the match.
- [ ] **b.** She hurt her foot during the match.
- [ ] **c.** She wants to stop playing football.

C **The girl in Activity B always wakes up late.** What advice would you give her? Use *should* and *shouldn't*.

1. She should use an alarm clock.
2. ______________________________.
3. ______________________________.

A **Label the picture.** What can you do in this room?

brush my teeth | shampoo | soap | toothbrush | toothpaste | towel

1. ______________
2. ______________
3. ______________
4. ______________
5. ______________
6. In this room I can ______________.

B **Read.** Circle the correct words.

Clean Birds

We have a shower every day and wash with soap and shampoo. We use a [1.] *jumper / towel* to get dry and we [2.] *brush / wash* our teeth with a toothbrush and some toothpaste. Animals have their own ways of staying clean.

Some [3.] *birds / giraffes* have 'dust baths'. They roll on the ground to take off the dirt and insects, and then they shake the dust off their bodies. Most birds also use their [4.] *hands / beaks* to get dust and insects out of their feathers. They use [5.] *oil / soap* from their bodies to clean the feathers too. Birds have about 25,000 feathers, so it's not an easy job!

But why do they do it? Because it keeps their feathers [6.] *strong / weak*, and the oil stops them from getting wet.

Oxpeckers are birds that like to clean other animals. They live in Tanzania, Africa, and they eat insects from the [7.] *feathers / fur* of giraffes. This helps to keep giraffes healthy. Sometimes, the oxpeckers clean the giraffes' ears! They take small pieces of food from between their [8.] *eyes / teeth* too. They also clean other animals like zebras, rhinos and buffaloes.

C **Correct the sentences.**

1. Birds clean their fur with oil. ______________________________
2. Oxpeckers live in Asia and Europe. ______________________________

A **Read the questions.** Write the answers in order.

1. Why should you eat fruit? it / because / full of / is / vitamins

____

2. Why do people run in the park? is / good / because / for you / exercise

____

3. Why is it important to brush our teeth? keeps / healthy / them / it / because

____

4. Why shouldn't you eat lots of sugar? your teeth / it's / for / because / bad

____

B **Look and write questions.**

1. children / resting
Why are the children resting?

3. girl / happy
____

2. man / awake
____

4. living room / dark
____

C **Answer the questions in Activity B.** Use *because* and your ideas.

1. Because they are hot after playing football.
2. ______________________________
3. ______________________________
4. ______________________________

Lesson 5 Writing

A **Your friend plays computer games too much and sometimes forgets to do homework.** What advice can you give? Complete the chart with ideas and reasons from the box.

You should do your homework before you play.	You need to have other hobbies.
You can take some exercise.	You shouldn't play computer games so much.
You should go outside.	Homework is very important.

Idea	1. ______	2. ______	3. ______
Reason	1. ______	2. ______	3. ______

B **Use your notes from the Unit 6 Writing Lesson to help you write three text messages giving advice.**

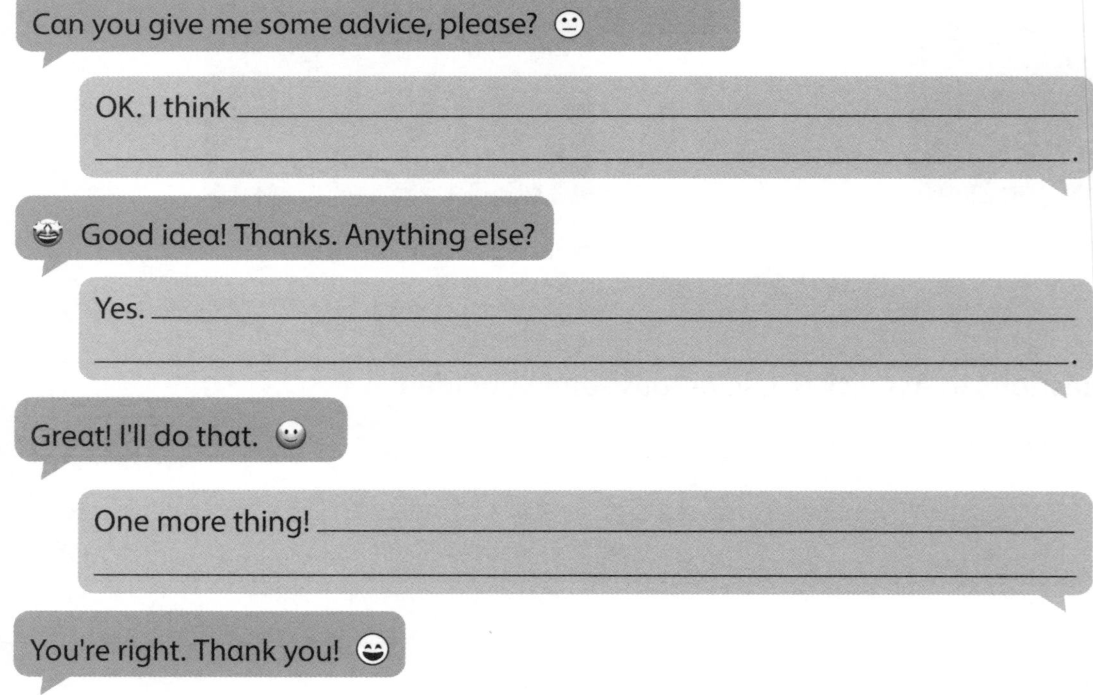

A **Take the Big Nature Quiz.** Circle the correct answer.

1. You can find elephants in ...

   a. Africa. b. Asia. c. Africa and Asia.

2. Whales are ...

   a. fish. b. mammals. c. insects.

3. Snakes in the Sahara desert sleep in the day because of ...

   a. the heat. b. the cold. c. the light.

4. Cows eat ...

   a. birds and small mammals. b. fish and insects. c. plants and grass.

5. Which animals don't live in the Arctic?

   a. polar bears b. seals c. penguins

6. Which animal is at the top of its food chain?

   a. a lion b. a mouse c. a kangaroo

7. Which is heavier – a tiger or a giraffe?

   a. a tiger b. a giraffe c. tigers are as heavy as giraffes

8. Most leaves need ...

   a. a little sun. b. lots of sun. c. no sun.

A humpback whale

B **Write two more questions for the Big Nature Quiz.** Use the information from Unit 6 Lesson 3 of the Workbook and the Student's Book.

1. ______________________________

   a. __________ b. __________ c. __________

2. ______________________________

   a. __________ b. __________ c. __________

A **Listen to the conversation.** What's the problem? Tick the correct answer. TR: 6.3

- [ ] **a.** The girl's bag is heavy.
- [ ] **b.** The girl hurt her leg.
- [ ] **c.** The girl can't find her coat.

B **Listen again and complete the conversation.** TR: 6.4

Pablo: Let me help! 1. ______________ your books for you, Anna?

Anna: 2. ______________. They aren't heavy – but it's difficult to carry them.

Pablo: How did you break your leg?

Anna: I was running in the rain. The ground was really wet and I fell.

Pablo: Ouch!

Anna: 3. ______________ my coat for me, please? It's there, on the chair.

Pablo: 4. ______________!

Anna: Thank you, Pablo.

Pablo: 5. ______________.

C **Look at the pictures.** Write conversations.

1\.

A **Match each piece of technology with the way it is used in the video to study lions.**

B **Complete the sentences about the pictures in Activity A.**

a drone	a robot with wheels	a truck with lights
at night	close to the lions	from above

1. When the lions are playing together, photographers use ________________ to take photos ________________.
2. When the lions are walking near the water, photographers use ________________ to take photos ________________.
3. When the lions are resting, photographers use ________________ to take photos ________________.

C **Imagine you have a robot camera and you go outside near where you live.** Answer the questions and draw a picture.

What animals can you see?

I can see ________________

________________.

What are they doing?

They are ________________

________________.

A Circle the correct words.

1. My cousin is very *strong* / *weak* – he carries all the shopping upstairs!
2. We have to be quiet because the baby is *asleep* / *awake*.
3. My bedroom window is very big, so it's very *dark* / *light* in my room.
4. When you feel ill, you should *rest* / *take exercise*.

B Complete the sentences.

app   charge   online   VR headset

1. When you want to find information, you can go ____________________.
2. Some people get an ____________________ on their mobile phone to learn English.
3. With some computer games, you can wear a ____________________ – it's like you're in the game!
4. If you can't turn on your tablet, you probably need to ____________________ it.

C Listen and tick the correct picture. TR: 6.5

1. Why is Tom asleep?

a. 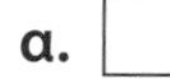 b. ☐ c. ☐

2. Where is the woman's e-book?

a. ☐ b. ☐ c. ☐

3. What advice does the boy give the girl?

a. ☐ b. ☐ c. ☐

D **Read and write advice with *should* and / or *shouldn't*.**

1. I want to eat a healthy snack.

   You should eat fruit or nuts. You shouldn't eat biscuits.

2. The students are taking a test tomorrow.

   ____

3. Your sister forgot her homework on the bus.

   ____

4. You are having problems sleeping at night.

   ____

5. Your best friend is crying.

   ____

6. You want to be a faster runner.

   ____

7. Your friend Tom is always late for school.

   ____

E **What will schools be like in the future?** Answer the questions using *will* or *won't*.

1. Will there be teachers in the future?

   ____

2. What will robots do?

   ____

3. Will there be laptops or books?

   ____

4. Will there be interactive whiteboards?

   ____

7 The City

Lesson 1 Vocabulary

A Complete the sentences. There are three extra words.

airport	bus station	hotel	fire station	pharmacy
police station	railway station	restaurant	square	university

1. After you finish school, if you want to study more you can go to a ________________.
2. When you don't feel well and you need medicine, go to a ________________.
3. When you want to fly to another city or country, go to the ________________.
4. When people go on holiday, they often stay in a ________________.
5 When you feel hungry, you can go to a ________________.
6. When you have a serious problem, you should go to the ________________.
7. You can often see monuments in the main ________________ of a city.

B Listen and label the map. Use the words from the box in Activity A. TR: 7.1

C Write about the area where you live. Use five or more words from the box in Activity A.

I live in ________________. Next to my house, ________________
and across the road ________________.
When I go to school, I go past ________________.
There isn't ________________.

A **Write the past participles of the verbs.**

Regular		Irregular	
play	played	make	______
climb	______	see	______
visit	______	eat	______
start	______	be	______

B **Complete the postcard.**

I've eaten	I've stayed	it has changed	they've built
we've been	we travelled	we haven't been	we haven't decided

Hello!

My sister is studying at a university in Rio de Janeiro and 1. ______ by plane to see her. She wants to be a doctor and she works in a pharmacy, but 2. ______ to see her at work yet – maybe next week!

My mum grew up in Rio, but she says 3. ______ a lot since the Olympic Games. 4. ______ a bigger airport, so we could fly directly from our city.

Our hotel is fantastic! It's the biggest hotel 5. ______ in. 6. ______ to lots of different restaurants and 7. ______ some traditional food. We want to visit some attractions tomorrow, but 8. ______ where to go. We'll read our guidebook tonight and decide!

See you soon!

C **Jamie and his friends are doing a project about their city.** Look at the list and write sentences. What have they done?

✓ write about the new airport (Jamie)

✓ take a photo of the old fire station (Alicia)

✗ finish the story about the hotel (Paco and Carmen)

✓ make a model of the square (Vera and Jenny)

1. Jamie has written about the new airport.
2. ______
3. ______
4. ______

Lesson 3 Reading

A **Write the words.**

1. o ________________
   b ________________
2. c ________________
3. m ________________
4. c ________________
   c ________________

B **Read and put the text in order.**

Unforgettable Cities

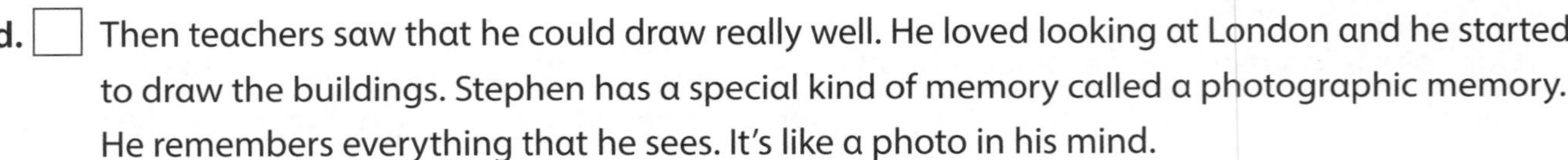

a. ☐ He has drawn London, Mexico City, Istanbul and New York. In this photo, Stephen is drawing Mexico City. He hasn't finished it, but he has drawn most of the city centre.

b. ☐ Later the same day, he starts to draw. He can remember the number of windows, floors and chimneys on each building!

c. ☐ Stephen also draws 3D pictures. He wears a VR headset and draws the shapes in the air!

d. ☐ Then teachers saw that he could draw really well. He loved looking at London and he started to draw the buildings. Stephen has a special kind of memory called a photographic memory. He remembers everything that he sees. It's like a photo in his mind.

e. ☐ Stephen has visited many cities around the world. Sometimes, he flies in a helicopter to see the city. He looks at the office buildings and the skyscrapers, the motorways and the parks.

f. ☐ When Stephen Wiltshire was young, he couldn't communicate well. He said his first word (*paper*) when he was five.

C **Complete the sentences with words from the text.**

1. The first time Stephen spoke, he said the word ________________ .
2. His ________________ saw his drawings and thought they were very good.
3. Stephen has a __________________________, so he remembers everything he sees.
4. Stephen sometimes goes in a ________________ to see the buildings from above.
5. He uses a ________________ to draw 3D pictures.

A **Read the conversation.** Write the questions (1–5).

Dad: Don't forget we're going out for dinner tonight!
1. ______________________________? (you / tidy / room)

Boy: a. ______________. I'll go and do it now.

Dad: Good idea. Oh, 2. ______________________________?
(sister / take / dog for a walk)

Boy: b. ______________. She took the dog out before school.

Dad: Great. And 3. ______________________________? (brother / take out / rubbish)

Boy: c. ______________. I can do it later.

Dad: Thank you. 4. ______________________________? (you / finish / homework)

Boy: d. ______________. We did it when we came home from school.

Dad: Excellent! OK, let's go. I'm hungry. I think I'm going to have a pizza.
5. ______________________________? (you / decide / what to eat)

Boy: e. ______________. I'll decide when we get to the restaurant.

B **Listen to the conversation in Activity A.** Write the boy's answers (a–e). TR: 7.2

C **Answer the questions.** Write *Yes, I have* or *No, I haven't.*

1. Have you travelled to many different countries? ______________
2. Have you decided what you want to be in the future? ______________
3. Have you studied English for more than five years? ______________
4. Have you visited a fire station? ______________

D **Write questions about your friends and family.** Find out the answers.

1. Has Grandma camped on a beach?

   No, she hasn't.

2. ______________________________

   ____

3. ______________________________

   ____

Lesson 5 Writing

A Read. Complete the chart with information from the poster.

Film Club

Do you love going to the cinema?
Are you excited about new films?
We're a group of friends who love watching films. We meet every Friday evening to go to the cinema. After the film, we talk about what we liked or disliked about it.
It's €10 a month. Don't forget to bring money for popcorn!
Talk to the drama teacher to find out more.

Questions	Photos
__________	__________
__________	__________
__________	__________
What and Who?	**When?**
__________	__________
__________	__________
__________	__________

Poster for
____
____

B Use your notes from the Unit 7 Writing Lesson to help you create a poster about your city.

__________ the Amazing City of __________

____________________?

____________________?

____________________?

We're __________ and we __________.

We meet ____________________.

____________________.

____________________!

____________________.

A **Read and answer the questions about your city.**

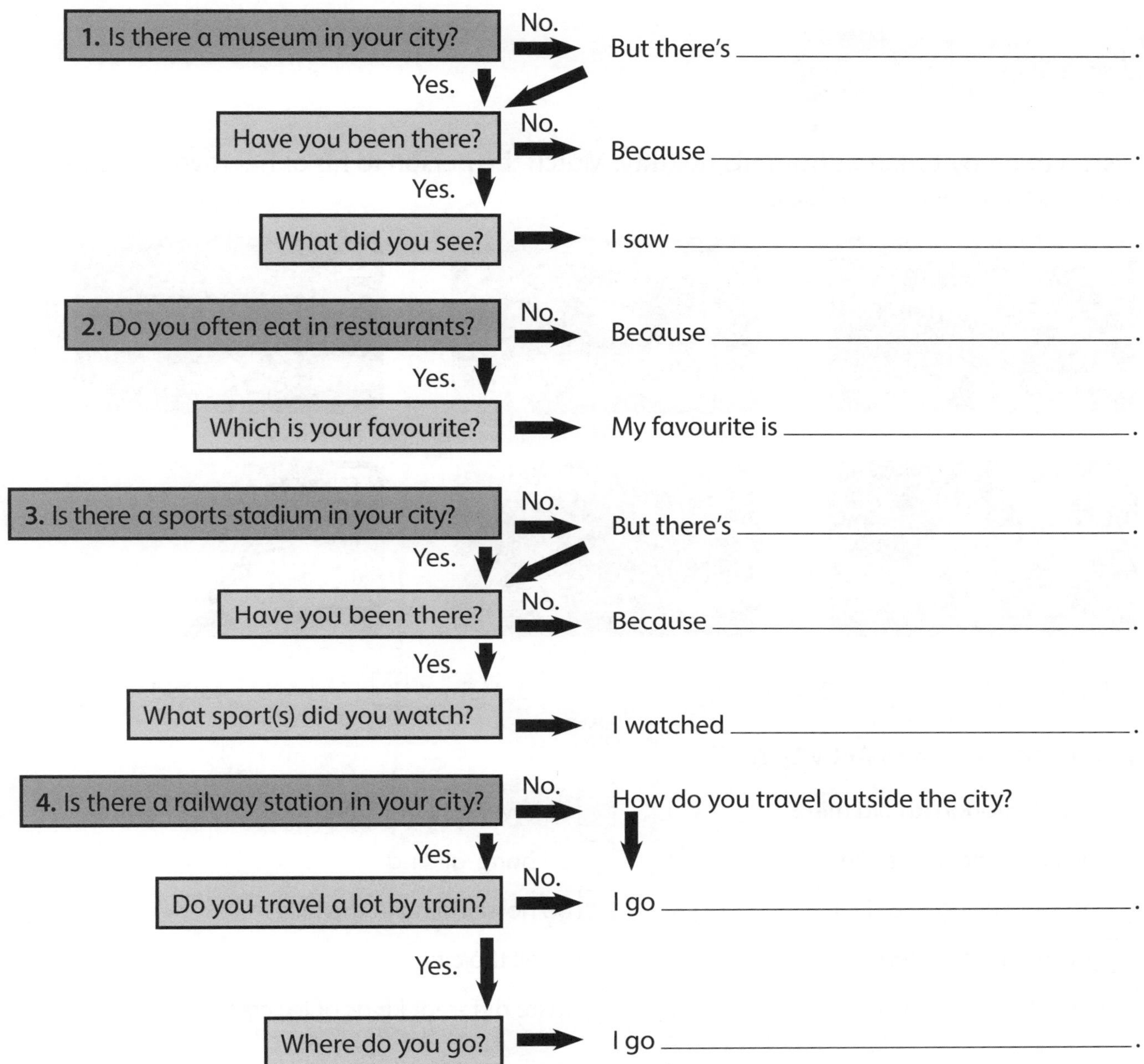

B **Have you visited a new place recently?** Show a photo of the place to your classmates and answer the questions.

1. Where did you go? ______
2. Did you like it? Why? / Why not? ______
3. Would you like to go there again? ______

8 You Can Do It!

Lesson 1 Vocabulary

A **Listen to a boy talking about his holiday.** Match the person to his or her favourite activity. There are two extra activities. TR: 8.1

a. b. c.

d. e. f.

1. Sam ☐ **2.** sister ☐ **3.** Mum ☐ **4.** Dad ☐

B **What can you see in Activity A?** Tick.

☐ crawl through an old mine
☐ go kayaking in the sea
☐ go snorkelling in a river
☐ jump off giant steps
☐ swing across a river
☐ discover a secret cave
☐ go hang-gliding
☐ go horse riding in the hills
☐ smell the city
☐ taste different kinds of ice cream

C **Answer the questions.** Use Activity B.

1. Which activities have you done? ______________________

2. Which would you like to try? ______________________

3. Which do you think would be difficult? ______________________

4. Which do you think would be exciting? ______________________

5. Which do you think would be scary? ______________________

A Match the questions and answers.

1. Have you ever drunk tomato juice?
2. Have you ever been horse riding?
3. Has your sister ever played an instrument?
4. Has your mum ever eaten chillis?
5. Has your brother ever seen a lion?
6. Has your dad ever lived in a different country?

a. Yes, he has. He studied at a university in Scotland.
b. No, she hasn't. She doesn't like spicy food.
c. Yes, I have. We had some in a market when we were in Turkey.
d. Yes, he has. He went to the zoo last week.
e. Yes, she has. She was in an orchestra when she was younger.
f. No, I haven't, but I've ridden a camel!

B Complete the questions with the present perfect and *ever*.

go camp climb play

1. ______________ to a rainforest?
2. ______________ in the snow?
3. ______________ a mountain?
4. ______________ in the countryside?

C Write sentences about your family and friends. Use Activity B.

1. My mum hasn't been to a rainforest, but she has climbed a mountain.
2. ______________
3. ______________
4. ______________

Lesson 3 Reading

A **Complete the sentences with the words.**

coast hide skills splashed

1. My brother ______________ me in the swimming pool yesterday.
2. This summer, we're going on holiday to a village on the ______________.
3. When you try a different sport, you have to learn new ______________.
4. We have to ______________ the presents so she doesn't see them before the party!

B **Complete the text with the animals Sophie saw.**

albatross humpback whale parrot fish red-footed booby sea lions

Exploring the Galapagos Islands

Some children have travelled to the Galapagos Islands as National Geographic Global Explorers. These children have seen many different animals and they've learnt new skills. This is what Sophie Lenoir experienced in the Galapagos Islands.

She saw amazing [1] ______________ on all the beaches along the coast. She saw a [2] ______________ for the first time. It jumped and splashed its tail. One day, she went to Genovesa Island. There were thousands of sea birds all around her there. They didn't hide, so she could see them really easily. Her favourite bird was the [3] ______________. It has a blue beak and red feet.

Another day, she went to Española Island and she saw an [4] ______________. Albatrosses are huge birds.

She learnt how to drive the ship, *Endeavour II*. She drove it across the equator. It was very exciting. She also saw many kinds of fish. Her favourite was the [5] ______________. It has a mouth like a parrot's beak. She learnt a lot about our beautiful planet. She wants to go back there one day.

C **Read the text again.** Correct the sentences.

1. Sophie saw sea lions in the water. ______________
2. The red-footed booby has a green beak. ______________
3. An albatross is a small bird. ______________
4. Sophie's favourite fish was the lion fish. ______________

A Listen to the girl. Tick the things her mum has done. TR: 8.2

1. go to Asia ☐
2. fly to Spain ☐
3. eat snails ☐
4. visit the pyramids in Egypt ☐
5. see a giant sea turtle ☐
6. ride a horse in Tunisia ☐

B Complete the sentences. Use the present perfect or the past simple of the verbs in parentheses.

1. She ______________ to Asia, but she's flown to countries in Africa, South America and Europe. (go)
2. When she went to Spain, she ______________ snails. (eat)
3. When she was in Mexico, she ______________ an old pyramid. (climb)
4. She ______________ the Egyptian pyramids, but she's going to next month. (visit)
5. She ______________ a giant sea turtle, but she ______________ any sharks. (see)
6. Last month, she ______________ horse riding in Tunisia. (go)

C Answer the questions. When you answer *yes*, give more information using the past simple.

1. Have you ever visited a big city in your country? ______________________________

   When did you go? ______________________________

   What did you do there? ______________________________
2. Have you ever travelled by boat? ______________________________

   Where did you go? ______________________________

   What could you see from the boat? ______________________________

Lesson 5 Writing

A **Read.** Complete the chart with information from the survey.

My Survey

I asked eight of my friends about sports and hobbies.

I used these questions:

1. Have you ever played basketball?
✓✓✓✓

2. Have you ever been horse riding?
✓✓✓

3. Have you ever painted a picture?
✓✓✓✓✓✓✓✓

4. Have you ever tried snorkelling?
✓

Question 1: ____________________
Number of 'yes' ____________________

Question 2: ____________________
Number of 'yes' ____________________

Survey
Who? ____________________
Topic: ____________________

Question 3: ____________________
Number of 'yes' ____________________

Question 4: ____________________
Number of 'yes' ____________________

B **Use your notes from the Unit 8 Writing Lesson to help you write a report about your survey.**

Survey on ____________________

I asked ____________________ about ____________________.

They are ____________________. I used these questions.

1. ____________________
2. ____________________
3. ____________________
4. ____________________

My Report

I counted the Yes answers and here are the results: ____________________

____

A **Look at some more challenges Dan and Seb Raven-Ellison did.** Which have you done? Put a tick in the box. Which would you like to do in the future? Put a ☺ in the box.

- ☐ dance at a festival
- ☐ draw birds
- ☐ climb a mountain
- ☐ collect 60 green things
- ☐ hide in a forest
- ☐ make your own bread
- ☐ make a micro-museum
- ☐ sleep on a beach
- ☐ stand behind a waterfall
- ☐ see a whale

Dancing in a festival, Philippines

B **Choose one of the challenges from Activity A.** Answer the questions.

1. Which challenge did you choose? ______________________________

2. Do you need an adult to help you? ____________

If you answer *yes*, who can you ask to help you? ______________________________

3. Can you do the challenge at home? ____________

If you answer *no*, where do you need to go? ______________________________

4. Do you need special clothes or equipment? ____________

If you answer *yes*, what do you need? ______________________________

5. How much time do you think the challenge will take? ______________________________

A **Write the words.**

1. You go here to buy medicine when you're sick.
2. This is the opposite of *awake*.
3. It's on the roof and smoke comes out of it.
4. You use this to wash your hair.
5. You put toothpaste on this when you brush your teeth.
6. When you finish school, you can study here.
7. This is the opposite of *weak*.
8. You do this sport on water.
9. You go here when you want to travel to a different city or country by plane.
10. This is an area in the city where people can meet and go to a café.
11. This is the opposite of *dark*.
12. You can go here for lunch or dinner.
13. You use your nose to do this.
14. You should use this when you wash your face and hands.
15. You use your mouth to do this.

B **What's the secret message?** Tick the photo that shows it.

______________________________!

The City at the End of the World

A Listen and tick the things you can do in Ushuaia. TR: 8.3

- [ ] see where the Atlantic and Pacific Oceans meet
- [ ] learn about Ushuaia's history at the End of the World museum
- [ ] try traditional Argentine barbecue in a restaurant
- [ ] swim to Martillo Island
- [ ] see penguins on Martillo Island
- [ ] take a boat tour to see humpback whales
- [ ] go skiing at Glacier Martial
- [ ] visit the Tierra del Fuego National Park

Magellanic penguins, Argentina

B Circle the correct answer.

1. Ushuaia is a city on an island in __________.
   a. Brazil　b. Argentina　c. Peru
2. Skyscrapers, large office buildings and __________ cannot be found in Ushuaia.
   a. motorways　b. hotels　c. houses
3. __________ is the best time to visit Ushuaia.
   a. Spring　b. Winter　c. Summer
4. You can see __________ different species of penguins on Martillo Island.
   a. two　b. three　c. four
5. Glacier Martial is near __________.
   a. the airport　b. Martillo Island　c. the town centre
6. The weather in winter is cold and __________.
   a. windy　b. snowy　c. rainy

C What activity would you most like to do in Ushuaia? Why? Draw a picture and write.

I would most like to ____________________

____

because ____________________

____________________.

A **Circle the one that doesn't belong.** Explain why.

1. airport | pharmacy | bus station | railway station

____

2. go kayaking | go snorkelling | swing across a river | jump off giant steps

____

3. hotel | mountain | restaurant | pharmacy

____

B **Read the conversations and circle the correct answer.**

1. **Micaela:** Have you tried the new restaurant in town?
   Fiona:
   a. No, I wasn't.
   b. Yes, I could.
   c. Yes, I went on Friday.
2. **Micaela:** Is it next to the railway station?
   Fiona:
   a. No, it's across from the bus station.
   b. Yes, it has.
   c. It's very expensive.
3. **Micaela:** Did you have a nice lunch?
   Fiona:
   a. Yes! All the food tasted delicious.
   b. Yes, we have.
   c. The bread smelled great.
4. **Molly:** Have you ever been horse riding?
   Ahmed:
   a. Yes, I have.
   b. Yes, I went.
   c. Yes, I do.
5. **Molly:** When did you go?
   Ahmed:
   a. I went last year, when I was in France.
   b. I'm going next summer.
   c. I liked it a lot.
6. **Molly:** Was it difficult?
   Ahmed:
   a. Yes, it has been.
   b. No, it didn't.
   c. No, it wasn't.

C What have the people in the photos done? Use the present perfect.

camp on a beach | do 125 challenges | draw a city
go kayaking | go sand boarding | visit a museum

1. ______________________

2. ______________________

3. ______________________

4. ______________________

5. ______________________

6. ______________________

D Complete the questions. Use the present perfect of these verbs and *ever*.

build | live | play | see

1. ______________________ in an orchestra?
2. ______________________ a sandcastle?
3. ______________________ in a different country?
4. ______________________ a dolphin?

E Answer the questions in Activity D. Give more information.

1. Yes, I have. I played the violin in my school orchestra.
2. ______________________
3. ______________________
4. ______________________

Word List

Unit 1

bang
carry
cello
classical music
climb
concert
dancer
drums
flute
keyboard
pop music
shout
singer
violin

Unit 2

bracelets
comfortable
frighten
hurt
leggings
match
plain
pockets
spotted
striped
sunglasses
trainers
weak

Unit 3

the back
chalk
circle
downstairs
an entrance
a floor
the front
a gate
glass
a key
a lift
pavement
a roof
squares
upstairs

Unit 4

broccoli
cereal
a chilli
a courgette
fresh food
jam
junk food
lettuce
nuts
olives
seed
a strawberry
sweetcorn
weed

Unit 5

app
charge a tablet
control
drop
e-book
go online
headphones
interactive whiteboard
laptop
microphone
satellite
send a text
VR headset
Wi-Fi

Unit 6

asleep
awake
brush our teeth
dark
dry
light
rest
shampoo
soap
strong
take exercise
toothbrush
toothpaste
towel
weak
wet

Unit 7

airport
bus station
chimney
city centre
fire station
hotel
motorway
office building
pharmacy
police station
railway station
restaurant
square
university

Unit 8

coast
crawl
discover
go hang-gliding
go horse riding
go kayaking
go snorkelling
hide
jump off
skill
smell
splash
swing
taste

CREDITS

PHOTOS: 5 (tl) Mikkelwilliam/E+/Getty Images, (tc) KidStock/Blend Images/Superstock, (tr) Reinhard Eisele/Mauritius/Superstock, (cl1) Daniel Prudek/Shutterstock.com, (cl2) LukaM/Shutterstock.com, (c1) Straga/Shutterstock.com, (c2) Stockcreations/Shutterstock.com, (cr1) Randi Scott/Shutterstock.com, (cr2) Svariophoto/Shutterstock.com; **6** (tl1) Jim Dyson/Getty Images Entertainment/Getty Images, (tl2) Bill Reitzel/DigitalVision/Getty Images, (tl3) Avava/Shutterstock.com, (tl4) Craig Lovell/Eagle Visions Photography/Alamy Stock Photo, (tc1) Fitopardo.com/Moment/Getty Images, (tc2) Aryan Firouzbakht Photography/Moment/Getty Images, (cl1) PeopleImages/DigitalVision/Getty Images, (cl2) Blend Images - Mike Kemp/Brand X Pictures/Getty Images, (c) Alenavlad/Shutterstock.com, (br) Toru Yamanaka/Staff/AFP Images/Getty Images; **7** (tl) Kazuhiro Nogi/Staff/AFP Images/Getty Images, (tc) © Atsuo Takanishi Lab, Waseda University, Tokyo, Japan, (tr) AP Images/Paul Sancya; **8** © Souvid Datta; **9** (tl) Kokhanchikov/Shutterstock.com, (cl) Hadrian/Shutterstock.com, (cr) Cultura Creative RF/Alamy Stock Photo, (bl) Studio CP/Image Source/Getty Images, (br) Catherine Delahaye/Digital Vision/Getty Images; **14** Carolyn Jenkins News/Alamy Stock Photo; **15** Giovanni Rufino/Contributor/Disney ABC Television Group/Getty Images; **19** (tl1) Soru Epotok/Shutterstock.com, (tl2) Jatuporn Chainiramitkul/Shutterstock.com, (tr1) Twin Design/Shutterstock.com, (tr2) Semeniaka Aleksandr/Shutterstock.com, (cl1) Moroz Nataliya/Shutterstock.com, (cl2) Serhii Brovko/Shutterstock.com, (cr1) Peter Gudella/Shutterstock.com, (cr2) Nampix/Shutterstock.com, (br) Independent Birds/Shutterstock.com; **22** (tl1) James Hodgson/Alamy Stock Photo, (tl2) Juice Images/Cultura/Getty Images, (tr1) Johner/Superstock, (tr2) JG Photography/Alamy Stock Photo, (cl1) Digerati/Alamy Stock Photo, (cl2) Imfoto/Shutterstock.com, (cr1) Ian Francis Stock/Alamy Stock Photo, (cr2) Yurok/Shutterstock.com; **23** Alexey Shatrov/Shutterstock.com; **24** Enguang Zhu/Tao Images Limited/Alamy Stock Photo; **28** (tl1) S_derevianko/Shutterstock.com, (tl2) Linda Studley/Shutterstock.com, (tr1) Joe Gough/Shutterstock.com, (tr2) All For You Friend/Shutterstock.com, (cl1) 5 Second Studio/Shutterstock.com, (cl2) Ekaterina Kondratova/Shutterstock.com, (cr1) Dragon_Fly/Shutterstock.com, (cr2) Jukov Studio/Shutterstock.com; **29** Christopher Furlong/Getty Images News/Getty Images; **30** (tl1) Andy Crawford/Dorling Kindersley Media Library-DNU/Getty Images, (tl2) Julia Sudnitskaya/Shutterstock.com, (tr1) Ekaterina Markelova/Shutterstock.com, (tr2) David Prahl/Shutterstock.com; **37** Burke/Triolo Productions/The Image Bank/Getty Images; **40** Stephanie Aglietti/AFP/Getty Images; **45** (tr) Jose Luis Pelaez Inc/DigitalVision/Getty Images, (bl) Steve Debenport/E+/Getty Images; **46** MartinMaritz/Shutterstock.com; **47** (cl) Alistair Berg/DigitalVision/Getty Images, (cr) Ranta Images/Shutterstock.com, (bl) Anatoliygleb/Dreamstime.com, (br) Hero Images/Getty Images; **49** Ethan Daniels/Shutterstock.com; **55** Agustin Diaz/EyeEm/Getty Images; **56** (tl1) Grand Warszawski/Shutterstock.com, (tl2) Miya38/Shutterstock.com, (tr1) Luzimag/Shutterstock.com, (tr2) FotoDruk.pl/Shutterstock.com, (cr) Yuri Cortez/AFP/Getty Images; **58** (tl) Flashpop/DigitalVision/Getty Images, (b) Joanna Dorota/Shutterstock.com; **60** (tl) Alexandra Lande/Shutterstock.com, (tc) Zoran Photographer/Shutterstock.com, (tr) Thomas Northcut/DigitalVision/Getty Images, (cl) WaterFrame/Alamy Stock Photo, (c) Esther Reales Irastorza/EyeEm/Getty Images, (cr) Rosley Majid/EyeEm/Getty Images; **62** Claudio Contreras/Minden Pictures; **63** Jag_cz/Shutterstock.com; **65** AWL Images/Danita Delimont; **66** (bl) BasPhoto/Shutterstock.com, (bc1) Monkey Business Images/Shutterstock.com, (bc2) Altanaka/Shutterstock.com, (br1) Brooke Fasani/Stone/Getty Images, (br2) Stephen Barnes/Food and Drink/Alamy Stock Photo; **67** RoxiRosita/Moment/Getty Images; **69** (tl) Mohamed Alhwaity/Reuters, (tc) Stephen Simpson/DigitalVision/Getty Images, (tr) © Daniel Raven-Ellison/National Geographic Image Collection, (cl) Yuri Cortez/AFP/Getty Images, (c) Charlie Munsey/Corbis Documentary/Getty Images, (cr) Mark Ralston/AFP/Getty Images.

ILLUSTRATIONS: All illustrations are owned by © Cengage Learning, Inc.